GABRIELE D'ANNUNZIO, NIETZSCHE, AND THE UBERMENSCH

Art, Philosophy, and Politics in Italy

AUBREY SAVAGE

978-1-7638613-0-5

Gabriele D'Annunzio, Nietzsche, and the
Ubermensch: Art, Philosophy, and Politics in Italy

Aubrey Savage

© Aubrey Savage, 2025.

CONTENTS

PREFACE

This monograph presents a comprehensive analysis of the ideas of Gabriele D'Annunzio, one of history's most intriguing figures. Departing from mainstream interpretations of his life, this exploration is conducted through a Nietzschean perspective. Rather than emphasizing his connections with Mussolini, which often overshadow D'Annunzio's legacy, we focus on the influences of Nietzsche and the Symbolist movement.

Gabriele D'Annunzio, an esteemed Italian writer and poet, was significantly influenced by the philosophy of Friedrich Nietzsche. Nietzsche's ideas on the will to power, the concept of the Übermensch, and the rejection of traditional morality had a profound impact on D'Annunzio, thereby shaping his literary works and political activities.

D'Annunzio was particularly intrigued by Nietzsche's concept of the Übermensch, which he interpreted as a paradigm for a new type of human being who surpasses the constraints of conventional morality and societal norms. In his literary works,

D'Annunzio often portrayed his protagonists as superhuman figures driven by their passions and ambitions to achieve greatness.

Nietzsche's influence on D'Annunzio extended to his political activism. In 1919, D'Annunzio led a group of nationalist volunteers in a march on the city of Fiume (now Rijeka, Croatia), which had been promised to Italy in the Treaty of Versailles. D'Annunzio established a state in Fiume, known as the Regency of Carnaro, and governed it according to his vision of a Nietzschean society. The Regency of Carnaro was distinguished by its rejection of democracy and its focus on individual freedom and creativity. While often likened to anarchism, it is more appropriately compared to Nietzsche's views on politics, which various scholars describe as heroic individualism, radical aristocratism, or individualist anarchism.

It is evident that D'Annunzio's political ideology was incompatible with fascism, and he unequivocally rejected key fascist principles. Throughout his life, he expressed support for a wide range of political movements, from socialism to nationalism, but not fascism. His views often shifted in response to his personal and artistic interests, rather than adhering to a coherent political philosophy. His actions in Fiume, for instance, were driven more by his desire for personal glory than by a commitment to fascist ideology.

Though D'Annunzio's reputation has been adversely affected by Mussolini plagiarising his ideas and implementing them poorly, it is essential to recognise that D'Annunzio never endorsed fascism. D'Annunzio distanced himself from several key fascist principles. For instance, he did not support the fascist emphasis on racial purity or anti-Semitism, and he was known to have Jewish friends and collaborators. Furthermore, D'Annunzio was highly critical of Mussolini and the Fascist Party, particularly their authoritarianism and acceptance of violence and repression. As an unconventional individual with similarly unconventional acquaintances, he found fascism's rigid mass movement problematic. Despite his efforts to distance himself from fascism, the movement persistently sought to assimilate him, ultimately contributing to his demise.

To clarify, Mussolini significantly misrepresented D'Annunzio's ideas and aesthetics. Therefore, the full responsibility for the consequences of fascism and 'proto-fascism' is attributed solely to Mussolini. This stance does not imply that fascism should not be condemned; rather, we affirm that it should indeed be condemned. However, the accountability lies with Mussolini, as determined by the consensus of the public, who deemed him as an appropriate scapegoat. Consequently, D'Annunzio should be considered another victim of Mussolini, who appropriated some of his ideas and sought to exploit them.

Before Mussolini rose to power, Gabriele D'Annunzio had already made a name for himself as an influential and controversial figure. As a prolific writer and poet, D'Annunzio was a leading advocate of the Symbolist movement in Italian literature. Originating in France in the late 19th century, Symbolism emphasized the use of symbols to express the ineffable and mysterious aspects of human experience. D'Annunzio's literary works were characterized by their rich, sensual language and their exploration of the more obscure and enigmatic dimensions of human existence. D'Annunzio's early works, particularly his novel *Il Piacere* (*Pleasure*), were profoundly influenced by French Symbolist poets such as Charles Baudelaire and Paul Verlaine. These literary pieces delved into themes of sensuality, decadence, and the quest for meaning in an ostensibly meaningless world.

D'Annunzio's later works, particularly his plays, continued to explore Symbolist themes while incorporating elements of Italian tradition and mythology. For instance, his play *La Fiaccola sotto il Moggio* (*The Torch under the Bushel*) was inspired by an ancient Roman myth, and his play *La Nave* (*The Ship*) drew upon Italian Renaissance art and literature. D'Annunzio's Symbolist works are notable for their pioneering literary techniques, including stream of consciousness narration, interior monologues, and fragmented narratives.

D'Annunzio's life was characterized by numerous high-profile relationships and public disputes, which frequently obscured his literary and political accomplishments. The pinnacle of both his career and controversy was undoubtedly his bold military expedition to Fiume. Regardless, he remained an immensely popular and influential figure within Italian culture, serving as an inspiration to artists, writers, and politicians alike.

This monograph delves into the life and legacy of Gabriele D'Annunzio, tracing his journey from his early years as an aspiring writer to his contentious military endeavors and eventual decline. Through a thorough analysis of his works and their historical context, this study aims to illuminate the intricate and often contradictory nature of D'Annunzio, a central figure during one of the most compelling and tumultuous periods in Italian history.

GABRIELE D'ANNUNZIO, NIETZSCHE, AND THE UBERMENSCH

ART, PHILOSOPHY, AND POLITICS IN ITALY

> Men of intellect, educated in the cult of the beautiful, preserve a certain sense of order even in their worst depravities. The conception of the beautiful is, so to speak, the axis of their being, round which all their passions revolve.[1]
> – *Gabriele D'Annunzio*

The Prophet

Gabriele D'Annunzio, the Prince of Monte Nevus (Snowy Mountain), is not nearly as well-known today as Friedrich Nietzsche, but he was a giant during his lifetime. At the time D'Annunzio was born, Italy was a new nation. Its southern half (the Bourbon Kingdom of the Two Sicily's) was annexed to the northern kingdom of Piedmont, and D'Annunzio was only seven years old in 1870 when the French withdrew from Rome and the borders of Italy as we know them today were completed.[2] Italy was going through a volatile transition period, passing from the old world of tradition into the modern era.

In his day, D'Annunzio was considered the greatest Italian poet since Dante and was nicknamed "*Il Vote*"[3] (the Italian *vate* stems from the Latin *vates*, meaning a poet imbued with prophetic abilities). D'Annunzio's popularity was so immense that the founder of the Futurist school of art, Flippo Tommaso Marinetti, once wrote that "his gift for pleasing is diabolical."[4] Time has judged Gabriele D'Annunzio harshly, however, with critics casting aside D'Annunzio's literary achievements and branding him as a misogynist or even as a precursor to fascism. These accusations are unfounded and reveal complete naivety regarding both history and D'Annunzio's character.

D'Annunzio was a complex individual with a strong personality that is easily misunderstood, and whilst it may be justified to say that he harbored elitist sentiments, calling him a Fascist is simply inaccurate considering that he exhibited a general attitude of antipathy toward Mussolini. And while it is true that D'Annunzio was certainly not suited for monogamous relationships, there is nothing to indicate that he was in any way misogynistic or abusive towards women. On the contrary, his long-term partners were all strong women, well-versed in the arts and literature, and were as eccentric as he was. Leaving these judgments aside, however, D'Annunzio's personal life is irrelevant to the value of his philosophical ideas in any event, so rather than allowing his personality to overwhelm his achievements, we will conclude our discussion of this topic with a quote from D'Annunzio himself. In his *Libro segreto* (*Secret*

Book), D'Annunzio wrote: "I am unfaithful because of love, because of the art of love when I love to the death."[5]

D'Annunzio's primary philosophical influence was Friedrich Nietzsche. D'Annunzio advocated for Aristocratic Radicalism, as described previously in this book, in his writings. However, he also took Nietzsche's ideas one step further by actualizing them in the real world, which perhaps makes D'Annunzio more 'Nietzschean' than Nietzsche himself. Nietzsche wrote that he was searching "for human beings who could be my heirs; I carry something around with me, which cannot at all be read in my books – and for that I search the most beautiful and fertile soil."[6] D'Annunzio answered his call.

Nietzsche repeatedly reiterates that his philosophy is not one for the present but for the *future*. Nietzsche also believes that his philosophy will be born 'posthumously.' Moreover, it is beyond doubt that Nietzsche hopes to create new kinds of philosophers in the future through his ideas.[7] Gabriele D'Annunzio fully intended to live up to, and even surpass, Nietzsche's expectations, as is indicated by D'Annunzio's library in his home at the Vittori ale, where an edition of Nietzsche's works with D'Annunzio's personal annotations written in the margins survives.[8]

Whilst reading Nietzsche in the 1890s, D'Annunzio quickly recognized ideas that were already nascent in his own work.[9] He then became an Italian 'Nietzschean,' viewing modern civilization as a thin veneer that barely covered up the savage and violent human instincts […] This search for 'the man within' (or the "new man," as it was often stated) was typical of the *fin de siècle*, and D'Annunzio was one in a long list of writers who became obsessed with discovering the essence of human nature and human originality at a time when the entire direction of civilization seemed destined to submerge such originality in a sea of conformity or "massification."[10]

It is rumored that D'Annunzio identified so strongly with Nietzsche that when he heard of Nietzsche's tragic death, he completely broke down and sobbed like a child:

The woman with whom he was living at the time, and who loved him dearly, tried to console him with those platitudes which are as palliative for mental pain as the turning of a two-edged knife in a gaping wound. "Nietzsche was a superman, and he died mad," wailed the poet. "I believe that I shall finish up as he did. Now I want you to swear before God that if someday I go insane you will hide me, and never let the cruel world laugh at the decay of my great intellect. Swear it! Swear it!" […] and retired to his studio to write his "Hymn to Nietzsche."[11]

Given the fact that D'Annunzio was a poet, this close identification with Nietzsche is not surprising since

Nietzsche frequently refers to poetry in his works. For example, Nietzsche writes that "[f]or a genuine poet, the metaphor is not a rhetorical figure, but an image which stands in the place of something else, which it genuinely beholds in place of a concept."[12] Poetry then proceeds to become a lucrative ground for philosophical speculations, as Babette E. Babich explains:

> To give this another expression here: as poets speak, mixing the metaphors of one sense into those of another, so our bodies transfer (mix) the impulses from one sense, apprehending the one sensation on the terms of another. Nietzsche's talk of "hearing with one's eyes" in *Thus Spake Zarathustra* reflects the same early emphasis.[13]

D'Annunzio understood the fluid nature of symbolism just as Nietzsche did. Certainly, both authors possessed many shared interests, including music, the arts, philosophy, and classical Greece. Like Nietzsche, he was no friend of the masses and periodically withdrew from society to write and study, electing to spend his spare time with his long-term female partners, horses, or dogs. Despite his enormous popularity, D'Annunzio was reclusive by choice.

The Beautiful Era

D'Annunzio was inspired by new ideas emerging from *La Belle Époque* (The Beautiful Era), which is the name sometimes given to the period between 1871 and 1914. This era was one of transition for Europe, and it produced several notable art movements such as Cubism, Art Nouveau, Literary Realism, Symbolism, and the Decadent. It was a creative pinnacle for Europe, but as much as it heralded the birth of new innovations, the era was also marked by tragedy: it was also the *fin de siècle* (End of the Century). Despite being the apex of creation, it was also associated with ennui, pessimism, and nostalgia. These forces would shape not only D'Annunzio's mindset but also the cultural *Zeitgeist,* which he would later embody.

D'Annunzio's first novel, *Il Piacere* (*The Child of Pleasure*), is heavily indebted to À *Rebours* (*Against Nature*) by Joris-Karl Huysmans, a work associated with both Symbolism and the Decadent movement. In À *Rebours* the main character, Jean des Esseintes, is an eccentric antihero who loathes 19th-century bourgeois society and is on a mission to create his own perfect aesthetic. Besides this, it also influenced D'Annunzio's taste in art, for it is well known that he was extremely indulgent when it came to unusual artifacts and antiquities and had an intense compulsion to buy not only the most beautiful, but also the most exotic items. Like Huysmans, D'Annunzio saw literature as a tool for progress that could advance society into the new century, aesthetically and culturally. Moira M. Di Mauro-Jackson suggests that *Il Piacere* is a type of socio-political manifesto for D'Annunzio: "*Il Piacere* is truly a breviary, to borrow Cevasco's term, a bible – or in socioeconomic terms, a manifesto – for its time."[14] Furthermore, even

D'Annunzio "calls his work a manifesto, a breviary of the elegant corruption of his century, a nostalgic last look at the dandy era that would be no more."[15] Close connections between art, philosophy, and politics were not unusual then, and as Marinetti reminds us, both "André Breton and Guy Debord also used their art to reshape the political power structure."[16] It is, therefore, here, at this preliminary stage of his thought, that D'Annunzio begins to postulate his own political ideas. According to Mauro-Jackson,

> [l]ike Huysmans' des Esseintes, D'Annunzio's hero is also the dying type representing the end of his era. Despite his name, Sperelli, from *speranza*, he is hopeless. Underscoring this irony, D'Annunzio refers to him as the "*ultimo discendente d'una razza intelletuale*" [the last descendant of an intellectual race] and again as belonging to a disappearing class of Italian nobility, "*quella special classe di antica nobiltà italica [che sta] scomparendo.*"[17]

The relationship between social decay and descent from nobility is a common theme of the Decadent movement. D'Annunzio's intent to influence politics is therefore declared in *Il Piacere*, where it portrays how D'Annunzio created his own type of propaganda or a "new type of politics that would efface the distinction between private and public, society and state."[18] D'Annunzio, by emphasizing the decadence in the old aristocratic world, is not attempting to bring about the demise of the aristocracy; instead, he attempts to *redefine* aristocracy, placing his political persuasion within the sphere of Aristocratic

Radicalism. This preference for aristocracy, but also the belief that its power is on the wane, is illustrated in *The Child of Pleasure*, where D'Annunzio writes, "The grey deluge of democratic mud, which swallows up so many beautiful and rare things, is likewise gradually engulfing that particular class of the old Italian nobility in which from generation to generation were kept alive certain family traditions of eminent culture, refinement, and art."[19] D'Annunzio also describes the character Sperelli's aristocratic lineage:

> To this class, which I should be inclined to denominate Arcadian because it shone with the greatest splendor in the charming atmosphere of the eighteenth-century life, belonged the Sperelli. Urbanity, Hellenism, love of all that was exquisite, a predilection for out-of-the-way studies, an aesthetic curiosity, a passion for archaeology, and an epicurean taste in gallantry were hereditary qualities of the house of Sperelli.[20]

D'Annunzio provides another description of an aristocrat in his short story "Giovanni Episcopo," where he writes that aristocratic lineage can be discerned in an individual by "a certain physical fitness, certain naturally elegant features, a certain cruelty, and certain complicated perfidies, and, besides, the instinct for sexual pleasure, the facile disgust, that very special way of wounding, crushing a person with a laugh – all these things and others revealed the presence of aristocratic blood."[21] Here again, though the physical appearance is refined, it also embodies decadence, and D'Annunzio attributes these characteristics to a vain woman who abuses her husband in a stark reversal of domestic violence's usual pattern. Her mother also physically assaults her father, so the description does not glorify the 'old aristocracy' but is rather a stark recognition of the aristocratic principle's decline.

With the advent of the 1900s, aristocratic power was on the wane, and decay had begun to set in. D'Annunzio's writings can be interpreted as a device to reinvigorate the failings of the aristocratic regime. To this extent, the book also has a redemptive element, namely the restoration of the aristocracy, in a new and vital form fit for the modern era. *Child of Pleasure*, therefore, concludes with a theme of redemption:

> Only once he is '*fin dentro la casa,*' [which are] the book's last words, do we realize that he [Sperelli] needs to die to let that new generation take over. He has buried himself alive, a living dead who cannot engage with the present or the future.[22]

D'Annunzio wishes to create "a new kind of aristocrat in the traditions of the Medici – connoisseurs and rulers – in order to create for himself a place in the ruling echelons of the country, in order to rise to the ruling class levels of Italian society."[23] *Il Piacere* offers a guideline for this. Later, D'Annunzio will also write that "[t]he true nobleman in no way resembles the spineless heirs of ancient patrician families."[24] Di Mauro-Jackson believes that D'Annunzio intended *Il*

Piacere to prepare people for a future world which would project

> [...] the *lettore futuro* into the new era, but not as an aesthetic movement, but a socio-cultural one. Suddenly, artists in Italy became politicians, because they had created a new kind of forward-looking "naturalism," incorporating not only the proletarian present of the increasingly failed *Risorgimento*, but also the great political and aesthetic resources available to Italians for a millennium.[25]

This new model of the "artist as politician" is entirely compatible with Nietzsche's vision of an ideal society presided over by artist-philosophers, which are the archetype for the Übermensch. Moreover, the concept of the Übermensch is consistent throughout D'Annunzio's writings and is far more than just a reoccurring theme, for some of the characters bear a staggering resemblance to D'Annunzio himself. One, therefore, must ask whether art is modeling life, or if life is intended to model art? D'Annunzio himself writes that "[o]ne must make one's own life as one makes a work of art," directly paraphrasing Nietzsche, who states that "[o]ne should fashion an unequivocal work of art out of one's own life."[26]

Canto Novo demonstrates that D'Annunzio is constructing an image for himself in which he becomes a 'Nietzschean superman.'[27] Another example of this is Hermil in *L'Innocente* (*The Innocent*), who speaks at length about "the excessive (*eccessivo*) development of his intelligence, his 'many-souled' qualities which nevertheless do nothing to modify 'the substantial basis of his being,' the hidden substratum, in which are inscribed 'all the hereditary characteristics of his race.'"[28] Paolo Tarsis is another literary superman in D'Annunzio's work, but who emphasizes war.[29] Stelio Effrena is the first D'Annunzian Übermensch who is free from the defects of his predecessors, who are defeated by their own sensuality;[30] however, there are still elements of this in Stelio, who is clearly in love with La Foscarina, but also lusts after Donatella. Stelio, who also appears in *The Flame of Life*, is clearly D'Annunzio himself, just as La Foscarina is a representation of his great love, the famous actress Eleonora Duse. As such, *The Flame of Life* should be regarded as a semi-autobiographical text, and thus Stelio's thoughts are likely identical to what the author thinks. D'Annunzio even goes so far as to explain this himself via Stelio:

> We can only obey the laws written in our own substance and by them we must remain complete in a fullness and unity that fill us with joy amongst so many dissolutions. There is no discord between my art and my life.[31]

This again refers to life and art in a similar way to the way Nietzsche approaches them. As Stelio is a manifestation of D'Annunzio's art, he is no different to – or separate from – the man who created him. Therefore, when Stelio describes his own personality, this is D'Annunzio's way of conveying his actual thoughts and feelings to the world. Thus, D'Annunzio describes his psychological state as driven by

The pride; the intoxication of his hard, dogged labor; his boundless, uncurbed ambition that had been forced into a field too narrow for it; his bitter intolerance of mediocrity in life; his claim to princely privileges; the dissembled craving for action by which he was propelled towards the multitude as to the prey he should prefer; the vision of great and imperious art that should be at the same time a signal of light in his hands and a weapon of subjection; his strangely imperial dreams; his insatiable need of predominance, of glory, of pleasure – rebelled tumultuously, dazzling and suffocating him in their confusion.[32]

There are two very important themes revealed here. One is that D'Annunzio's prime motivation is social recognition as channeled through his ambition, and the second is that he views himself as quintessentially different from the 'multitude' who are his 'prey.' At the point in his life when this book was composed, D'Annunzio was already a celebrity and quite capable of controlling the multitudes, but he was obviously aware that there was a distinction between himself and them. This 'influence over the Herd whilst remaining distant from the Herd' is a hallmark of Nietzsche's philosophy: in order to alter the masses, one must observe and participate and yet remain separate from them because to become one with them would render the Nietzschean philosopher inert; he would lose the vital essence that makes him creative, the very uniqueness which allows him to direct and change the flow of history, which is something that cannot be achieved by a person who does not possess the divine spark of creativity. In order to be creative, one must think differently. The fact that D'Annunzio refers to the multitude as 'prey' can also be seen as a reference to Nietzsche's 'Herd' metaphor.

As mentioned earlier, pleasure is a leading cause of the failure of D'Annunzio's previous Übermens*ch*. Perhaps, since the character of Stelio is based on himself, he wishes to remain impervious to this flaw in *The Flame of Life*. However, the idea of pleasure as a principal cause of decline is equally important as a philosophical concept to the plot. But we are given to fully understand why pleasure is the downfall of D'Annunzio's fictional Übermensch in *Il Piacere*, which adds a new layer of understanding to his philosophy:

> Another seed sown by the paternal hand had borne evil fruit in Andrea's spirit – the seed of sophistry. Sophistry, said this imprudent teacher, is at the bottom of all human pleasure or pain. Therefore, quicken and multiply your sophisms and you quicken and multiply your own pleasure or your own pain. It is possible that the whole science of life consists in obscuring the truth. The word is a very profound matter in which inexhaustible treasure is concealed for the man who knows how to use it. The Greeks, who were artists in words, were the most refined voluptuaries of antiquity. The sophists flourished in the greatest number during the age of Pericles, the Golden Age of pleasure.[33]

Thus, for D'Annunzio pleasure has a very strong connection to sophistry, demonstrating his intellectual prowess and understanding of philosophy. Again, we can see the realization of this in D'Annunzio's own life, in which his single greatest pleasure was the gratification of his Will. Other references D'Annunzio makes to philosophy are much more explicit. For example, D'Annunzio proudly proclaims Nietzsche as his literary inspiration when he, in a very unsubtle manner, introduces *Il Trionfo della Morte* (*The Triumph of Death*) with a direct homage to Nietzsche: "We bend our ear to the voice of magnanimous Zarathustra, O Ruler of the Convent; and we prepare in our art with certain faith, the advent of the Übermensch, the Superman."[34] References to Nietzsche are also obvious elsewhere in the book, such as when Giorgio reflects:

> Where breathes the human being to whom the whole day, from dawn to dusk, is a festival, consecrated by a new conquest? Where lives the dominating hero, crowned with the crown of laughter, that crown of smiling roses of which Zarathustra spoke? Where lives the strong, tyrannical dominator, free from the yoke of any false morality, sure in the feeling of his own power, convinced that the essence of his person overcomes in value all accessory attributes, determined to raise himself above Good and Evil by the pure energy of will, capable of forcing life to maintain its promises to him?[35]

In *Le Vergini delle Rocce* (*The Maidens of the Rocks*), references to Nietzsche take a different form and add another layer of complexity. D'Annunzio uses symbols that distinctly progress from Nietzsche's thought and are unique to D'Annunzio's literary style. Not only is the character of Claudio Cantelmo explicitly Nietzschean in this book, it is also worthwhile noting that

> [t]he three virgins, who are of royal blood, are represented as all "aiming at the infinite," each in a different way. Massimilla yearns to give herself in absolute self-sacrifice and gets her glimpses of the beauty of life as she is about to renounce it. Anatolia has visions of giving birth someday to a superman, and becoming the founder of a race of ideal men and women, while Violante, the mystic visionary, has in her dreams lived a thousand glorious lives, finding occult analogies with her own being and the most diverse things.[36]

Three different approaches to the ascension of humanity are thus described through their analogies with women: aesthetic, biological, and spiritual. Furthermore, this is an act of 'martyrdom' on behalf of the virgins, which takes on an obvious sacral dimension. The path of ascension is not restricted to the female characters, either, as is demonstrated when the male protagonist of the book, Claudio Cantelmo, says:

> The world is the representation of the sensitivity and thought of a few superior men,

who have created, amplified and adorned it during the course of time, and who will continue to amplify and adorn it more and more in the future. The world, as it appears today, is a magnificent gift donated by the few to the many, by the free to the enslaved, by those who think and feel to those who have to work.[37]

This statement is clearly Nietzschean, and we can find its precedent when Nietzsche writes that

[w]e the thinkers and sensitive ones are the ones who actually and continuously create and make something that is not yet there: the entire and eternally growing world of estimations, colors, accents, perspectives, steps of insight, affirmations, and denials. These poems invented by us are constantly learned and practiced by the practical humans (our actors, as indicated) who translate it into reality and the everyday world.[38]

The implication of this is that cultural impetus is derived from the few on behalf of the many, and as such, it is a process of mutual symbiosis; the few provide for the many, whilst the many support the few.

D'Annunzio did not exclusively write fiction, however; he was also a writer at the *Tribuna* newspaper, though he often used pseudonyms such as "Sir Charles Vere de Vere, Mario de' Fiori, Happenbucke, Shium-Sui, the Duke Junior, Marchese di Caulonia, Mab, Avelt, Lilla, Biscuit, etc."[39] This public profile and his connections to celebrities such as Eleonora Duse would eventually enable D'Annunzio to take his ideas from the theoretical level of literature and manifest them in a very real and tangible way when he entered the world of politics.

The Elective Beast

In the *Corriere di Napoli newspaper, which* was consistently critical of Italy's democratic institutions, D'Annunzio published an article in September 1892 entitled 'La Bestia Elettiva' (The Elective Beast), which dealt with both Nietzschean and Darwinian ideas.[40] In another article, D'Annunzio writes that

> [m]en will be divided into two races. To the superior race, which shall have risen by the pure energy of its will, all shall be permitted; to the lower, nothing or very little. The greatest sum of well-being shall go to the privileged, whose personal nobility makes them worthy of all privileges.[41]

This 'race' D'Annunzio speaks of is not based on superficial physical appearances or skin color – it is based on Nietzsche's concept of the *Will to Power*. Furthermore, D'Annunzio also wrote, "[h]istory belongs, above all, to the active and powerful man, the man who fights one great battle, who needs the exemplary men, teachers, and comforters and cannot find them among his contemporary companions."[42] Both of these statements harken back to Nietzsche's words on the polarization of men between those who would ascend or descend life, and it is those who ascend life who hold the most value for human civilizations because they possess the ability to bring about change on a large scale, improving and altering the world around them through the raw power of creation.

D'Annunzio's political exploits began simply enough when he ran as an independent candidate in a local election. However, nothing about D'Annunzio particularly embodied the mood or sentiment of bourgeois politics, and perhaps this is why this venture was doomed to failure. Despite achieving a certain amount of success in his first campaign, this experiment with politics did not eventuate as originally planned. As a candidate, D'Annunzio seems to have held a great deal of 'novelty value' for the average voter, but this was to wear off once the public realized that D'Annunzio was a tad too eccentric to ever really be a politician. Moreover, this disenchantment appears to have been completely mutual: D'Annunzio also lost interest in the voters. Actively participating in the democratic election process served to enhance his disgust for electoral procedures, as is revealed by comments he made in a letter to one of his publishers:

> I have just come back from an electoral trip, and my nostrils are still full of the acrid scent of humanity. This enterprise may seem stupid and extraneous to my art, but to judge my aptitude it is necessary to await the effect towards which my will is bent directly. Victory meanwhile is assured.[43]

From this one can surmise that D'Annunzio did not enjoy his own election campaign, even when he expected to win.

D'Annunzio's brief flirtation with democracy commenced on July 16, 1897, when he wrote a letter to Francesco Ercole (who was to become one of D'Annunzio's strongest supporters), confirming his willingness to run as a candidate to represent the coastal region of Ortona a Mare.[44] During this campaign, D'Annunzio first devised the "politics of poetry," a concept he would revisit later. Italian democracy, even at this formative stage, was essentially a simple model based on the heavily reductionist definitions of 'Left' and 'Right.' D'Annunzio did not conform to either definition and cannot be labeled as either because he clearly sought to control both political groups, taking ideas and drawing support from both when it suited his own agenda. As Lucy Huges-Hallett states, "He was not a party man, having far too lively a sense of his unique importance to subscribe to a program imposed by others."[45] Without democracy, there is neither a Left nor a Right, and if D'Annunzio did not believe in democracy, then both terms were meaningless to him. In light of this, D'Annunzio's primary objective was the establishment of his own system of governance. As such

> D'Annunzio's "political" thought was concerned with national greatness, the aesthetics of Italian cities, the creativity of the Italian people, and the virility of Italian men. His notion of "politics" was an essentially

spiritual one, and this was quite in keeping with the temper of the age. Many people agreed with D'Annunzio that parliamentary politics were banal or ignoble.[46]

A vote for D'Annunzio, then, was a protest vote against the State itself – and he won a seat in the Chamber of Deputies with this message. Thus, no one should have been surprised that even though D'Annunzio began his political career on the Right, he soon turned to the Left, because he had never professed allegiance to either side in the first place. Clarifying his lack of interest in party dogma, D'Annunzio stated that his fictional heroes "were all 'anarchists' intent on manifesting their will in bold actions."[47] Therefore, even though D'Annunzio had initially aligned himself with the monarchists and nationalists, when the government attempted to introduce repressive legislation, D'Annunzio crossed the parliamentary floor to sit on the Left. He wrote in his notebook that

> [o]n one side there are many dead men howling, and on the other a few men alive. As a man of intellect I advance towards Life.[48]

The use of the term 'Life' is significant, for as Nietzsche tells us, the Will to Power is the Will to Life, and in this sense of the word, Nietzsche capitalized the word *Leben* (Life) to distinguish everyday life (*Bios*) from idealized Life (*Zoë*); the two words for life in ancient Greek have separate meanings. D'Annunzio continues to use Life in a Nietzschean manner later, as a way to describe the drive for both cultural and personal ascension, saying that "[w]e have raised ourselves to the level of honorable thoughts; even more, we determine honor on earth, "nobility" – all of us are today advocates of Life."[49] The Will to Life admits the necessity of change and the heroic vitalism that conquers mundane life in order to achieve ideal Life. Therefore, with higher Life as his aim, D'Annunzio very deliberately crossed the floor to join the opposition. Gerald Griffin narrates the event:

> D'Annunzio sent out a statement to the press in which he contrasted the inertia and coma of the Right with the courage and drive of their opponents, and added that henceforth he would vote on the Socialist side. And so he did. The very next day he waited until the House was full, then he majestically rose from his seat on the Right and sauntered solemnly to a seat on the Left. It was just a pose with him. He had no political convictions of any kind.[50]

Considering the last sentence, D'Annunzio cannot be said to have 'betrayed' the Right, because he was never on either side to begin with. As Ledeen says, "In actuality these terms were virtually meaningless to D'Annunzio, for he was no more allied with the traditional Italian Right than with the Socialists."[51] D'Annunzio himself quite openly states that he was always an individualist, and he crossed the floor not because he believed in the Left, either, but because he was disgusted with the entire political process:

"Do you really think I'm a Socialist?", D'Annunzio asked a journalist two days later. "It pleased me to go for a moment into the lion's pit, but I was driven to it by my disgust with the other parties. Socialism in Italy is an absurdity […] I am and remain an individualist, fiercely and to the uttermost."[52]

Nonetheless, the Socialists were eager to embrace D'Annunzio, and his swing from Right to Left offered him the opportunity to stand as their candidate in Florence in 1900.[53] When Parliament was dissolved in June 1900, D'Annunzio stood for re-election in Florence but was defeated by conservative Tommaso Cambray-Digny.[54] Paradoxically, although this brought an end to his involvement in conventional politics, it was nevertheless only the beginning of his true political endeavors. As John Woodhouse writes, "The true nobleman, in D'Annunzio's sense, would never soil his hands with a voting slip, and so for the moment he had to renounce his rule."[55] Whilst he seemed genuinely surprised to have lost his seat, D'Annunzio does not appear to have regretted his loss due to his waning interest in mainstream politics. This was noted by Masci, who states in *La vita e le opera* (*Life and Work*) that D'Annunzio's

> first contacts with the electoral beast had made his hair stand on end. The enterprise, which had from a distance seemed tempting, now disgusted him.[56]

From this point on, D'Annunzio's involvement in politics would take a radical and most unexpected turn; having failed to maintain power within the democratic system, he was going to come to power independently of it – and his attitude became inherently, and often violently, revolutionary. D'Annunzio then had "no respect for the electorate, and no compunction about undermining the authority of democratic institutions."[57] He had always been an independent candidate, but he then claimed that "I am beyond Right and Left, as I am beyond good and evil."[58]

The Candidate for Beauty

During both his political campaigns, D'Annunzio referred to himself as the '*Candidato della Belleza*' (Candidate for Beauty), and his actual political affiliation was either unclear or non-existent.[59] 'Candidate for Beauty' may sound like an absurd title for a politician, but the reality is that D'Annunzio was simply being too clever for his own good. He wasn't just mocking Italian democracy with meaningless rhetoric; he did have a philosophical idea behind the term. The concept of beauty was as central to D'Annunzio's philosophy as it was to his aesthetic style as a writer. He wrote:

> The intellectuals trained in the cult of beauty always follow a systematic method of conduct even in their wildest aberrations […] The Concept of Beauty is the axis around which their very being revolves, and around this axis, their passions revolve too.[60]

This is further explained in *Il fuoco* (*The Flame of Life*), where Stelio states that

> the fortunes of Italy are inseparable from the fate of Beauty, of who she is the mother [...] Should not a new art, robust in both roots and branches, rise from ruins steeped in so much heroic blood, and should not this art sum up within itself all the forces latent in the hereditary substance of the nation? Should it not become a constructive and determining power in the third Rome, pointing out to the men who were taking part in its government the primitive truths to be made the basis of new forms?[61]

Beauty, according to D'Annunzio, is the force at the center of the Italian *Zeitgeist*, the true soul of its civilization, and the ultimate 'Ideal Form' of the Italian government. Thus, when he says he is the 'Candidate for Beauty', it is a poetic metaphor for the representative of the Ideal Form of Italy at its apex of civilization and culture – a concept which would have gone well over the head of the average voter. For D'Annunzio, politics is not about ideologies or parties, it is about culture and glory – all the factors which distinguish a grand civilization from a mediocre one. This is in line with Nietzsche's visions of 'Grand Politics', in which political parties no longer exist and are supplanted by leaders who function as a class or guild.

The emphasis D'Annunzio places on art is also evident in Nietzsche's philosophy. Nietzsche's Apollo/Dionysus dichotomy essentially revolves around two different creative aspects of humanity, both of which express a creative/artistic function. This begins in *The Birth of Tragedy*, which lays out the groundwork for Nietzsche's aesthetic theory and is later expanded on in terms of both religious and political philosophy, with the Dionysian function assuming dominance over that of the Apollonian and incorporating it within its own formless nature. Accordingly, the Übermensch is more akin to an artist than a contemporary politician because he creates culture instead of merely legislating it through bureaucratic procedure. D'Annunzio, as the Candidate for Beauty, is an artist in this sense of the term, as well as in the literary one.

D'Annunzio was destined to lead politics into previously uncharted waters, not only by utilizing Nietzsche's ideas but also by combining them with what he called the "politics of poetry." This term indicates that it is a "literature of politics" – not in the superficial sense of literature connected with a given party or sect, or a writer's effect on political life, but in the sense of a sustained reflection on the close links between political and poetic practices."[62] This link between poetry and politics becomes increasingly obvious as his public speeches progress, and D'Annunzio channels his literary skills into oratory with clear political objectives. At this point, D'Annunzio now also begins to incorporate mystic and symbolic elements into his speeches, utilizing religious rhetoric and claiming to see visions.[63] He now likens the relationship between the speaker and the crowd to that between the artist and his creation, an idea which is based on Nietzsche's description of the Übermensch. D'Annunzio writes that

> [t]he crowd contains a concealed beauty from which only the poet and the hero can obtain flashes [of inspiration]. When that beauty reveals itself in the unexpected noise that surges forth in the theatre or the piazza or the trench, then a torrent of joy swells the heart of the man who has inspired it with his verse, his oratory, or his sword. The word of the poet communicated to the crowd, like the gesture of the hero, is, therefore, an act that carries an instantaneous beauty in the obscurity of the soul, just as a sculptor can draw forth a divine statue from a block of stone...[64]

With this concept in mind, D'Annunzio's public orations start to take on the tone of what is now called 'propaganda,' which D'Annunzio deploys in a similar fashion to that espoused by Gustave Le Bon, and the 'passive' crowd is controlled by the 'active' leader. Again, this is like Nietzsche's Übermensch, as D'Annunzio

> allowed his public no break in his contrivance of their hysteria. He played on them with rhetorical tricks borrowed from the religious liturgy of classical drama. "Hear me!" he cried "Listen to me!" "Understand me!" [...] These were not speeches to be rationally appraised but acts of collective self-hypnosis.[65]

Directing the people's hatred against Italy's political leadership was a fundamental element of D'Annunzio's revolutionary speeches. His ability to motivate the masses can also be interpreted as a tactical deployment of Nietzsche's theories regarding *ressentiment*, wherein the oppressed elements of society overthrow their rulers. Though Nietzsche himself saw *ressentiment* as a dishonorable political stratagem, it has been the heart of every revolution throughout history. D'Annunzio was undoubtedly aware of Nietzsche's opinion of the politics of *ressentiment* but chose to deploy this strategy regardless.

Unlike many revolutionaries, D'Annunzio was successful in setting up his model of civilization – albeit it for a very limited time, during the period when he governed the city of Fiume. Whilst the Fiume experiment cannot be classified as an enduring system of government due to its brevity, it does allow us to see exactly what D'Annunzio's actual political beliefs were.

Sacred Entry

The historical circumstances which surrounded the events at Fiume were invested with both great unrest and a desire for progress. The Great War had recently ended and, following the Russian Revolution, revolt was very much in the air. This period of unrest coincided with cultural factors such as the *fin de siècle*, advancements in technology, and art movements such as Art Nouveau and Futurism, all of which combined to produce the 'perfect storm.' The world was changing at a rapid pace, and the seeds of revolution had been sown in Europe's fertile imagination. D'Annunzio was in the right place at the right time, and in possession of a very potent combination of talents: military prestige and aesthetics. The 'Candidate for Beauty' was going to show the world that he could also fight. D'Annunzio, in short, possessed the means to wage war simultaneously through culture and on the battlefield, as he demonstrated at Fiume.

The Slavonic name for Fiume is Rjeka, Riek, or Reka, and it was known to the Germans as St. Veit am Flaum.[66] The *Encyclopedia Britannica* states that the population of Fiume in 1900 was 38,955, comprising 17,354 Italians, 14,885 Slavs (Croats, Serbs, and Slovenes), 2,482 Hungarians, and 1,945 Germans.[67] Its population was, therefore, as much Italian as it was Slavic. In 1919 D'Annunzio, like many Italians, believed that Fiume, which was now up for grabs given that the Austro-Hungarian Empire had been dissolved, should come under Italy's sovereignty. For Italy, the importance of Fiume was primarily strategic. Ledeen tells us that "[b]y the time of the outbreak of the Great War, it was the major hub for the railroad lines leading to Belgrade, Prague, Budapest, and Zagreb, and was the natural outlet for commerce flowing between these cities and the West."[68] The newly-founded Kingdom of the Serbs, Croats, and Slovenes (which later became the Kingdom of Yugoslavia) made its own claim on Fiume, however. And while the matter of Fiume's fate was being debated by Allied politicians in France, D'Annunzio took matters into his own hands and seized control of the city, backed by a volunteer army of elite Italian war veterans drawn from the Arditi, on September 10.

During the period of his governance from September 1919 until December 1920, D'Annunzio conducted a unique experiment in political rule that stood as a model of anti-liberal politics.[69] The Arditi were heroes, and in "contrast to the foot soldiers who waited to die in a muddy trench, the Arditi died a 'beautiful death,' participating in desperate assaults on enemy positions, leading charges up exposed hillsides, singing (according to the legend) their own songs."[70] Following the war, the Arditi returned home, where they enjoyed hero status, while feeling purposeless in peacetime. D'Annnunzio's speeches on nationalism and revolution were a natural attraction for them, and the Arditi, no longer in the service of the government, became D'Annnunzio's personal army. Given that they were some of the more prestigious soldiers in Italy, this added a great deal of power to D'Annunzio's speeches. Léon Kochnitzky (a socialist poet and supporter of D'Annunzio) referred to the Arditi as "the dark seraphim of another Apocalypse."[71] And as Huges-Hallett writes, "The Arditi might not fit with that part of D'Annunzio's life which included Gothic bibelots, Murano glass and china tea, but he prized them as he had prized his greyhounds, for their physical splendor and their appetite for killing."[72] D'Annunzio's view of warfare was quite similar to that of the Arditi, and he once told Marcel Boulanger that "I adore war," and wrote to another friend, "For me and for you and for those like us, peace today is a disaster."[73] D'Annunzio knew what he was speaking about; he had been to war and returned with the medals and injuries to prove it. The Arditi and D'Annunzio were, therefore, mutually enamored with each other: they admired his leadership skills, and he admired their military prowess. They remained utterly loyal to each other despite all the events which unfolded at Fiume.

D'Annunzio's plans for Fiume were almost disrupted when he fell ill just before the march on the city. At dawn on September 12, he staggered up from his sick bed took his place at the head of 287 men, joking that he was "going to be shot when [he] returned."[74] Against all odds, D'Annunzio captured Fiume, and referred to this victory as his 'Sacred Entry' – the emphasis here was strongly placed on the religiosity of the experience and its essentially Dionysian character. With the Arditi perched precariously on the ledges along the palace facades, D'Annunzio delivered his inauguration speech to the people of Fiume:

> "Italians of Fiume," he began. "Here I am." He repeated himself insistently. "Here I am... Here is the man...*Ecce Homo*."[75]

This is an unmistakable reference to Nietzsche's book *Ecce Homo: How One Becomes What One Is*, and Nietzsche's art of becoming is essentially "[t]he invitation to become what one is an encomium, praising not one's human potential or possibility for being but what is already a consummate, measured achievement (if not for that a "conscious" one): thus it is one's conscience that says: 'Become the one you are!'"[76] The use of this phrase is not coincidental. It indicates that D'Annunzio perceived himself as having reached his full potential at Fiume.

During his reign at Fiume, D'Annunzio strongly emphasized holding festivals, providing a religious dimension to what would have otherwise been drab political events. Whilst this has been cited by some critics as evidence that he had no practical political agenda, it could also be argued that, on the contrary, the religious elements in D'Annunzio's political style were required to achieve his goal. Ledeen, for example, writes that because of the diverse nature of Fiume's population, the "regime demanded that the citizens be drawn together into an emotional unit that was, in turn, given a symbolic importance."[77] On the first anniversary of the Sacred Entry, D' Annunzio raised a new standard: a purple flag with gold stars framed by an Ouroboros (a serpent eating its own tail).[78] The Ouroboros, as stated previously, is a central element of Nietzschean symbolism. This demonstrates that, as D'Annunzio tells us, his greatest political achievement was that "I knew how to give my action the lasting power of the symbol."[79] This is precisely the same use Nietzsche had in mind for it in terms of revitalizing culture. D'Annunzio's use of symbolism would also come to the fore in his speeches at Fiume. The elements of his style

> were clear in his opening speech to the Fiumans: politics had become something greater, something transcendental. In his dialogue with the crowd, D'Annunzio

manipulated the mass of his listeners into a single personality, which spoke to him with a single voice. When he asked it for its act of faith, it spoke to him with a single *si*, and he expected this unanimity.[80]

D'Annunzio then shifted from being a political agitator and started to take on a role more akin to that of a Zarathustra-style prophet than a politician. This element is also present in his literature. In *Il fuoco*, D'Annunzio declares that he is aware of his oratory prowess when he speaks through Stelio:

> A not unseen miracle was now taking place within him, surprising his ear by the unforeseen cadence of the words that fell from his lips. An almost divine mystery was unfolding through the communion into which his soul had entered with the soul of the crowd. Something greater and stronger was adding itself to the feeling he had about his own person. And at every moment it seemed that his voice was acquiring a higher virtue.[81]

Through passages such as these, it is abundantly clear that D'Annunzio believed his speeches had a mystical aspect to them. Moreover, he shows in *Notturno* that he understood his own ability to manipulate crowds:

> I speak. Each of my words echoes under my skull as if cast back by domed metal. Each breath strains the circle of my breath. I suffer and am proud that my joy I mixed with pain. It is like the suffering of creation, like the

12. All the citizens of both sexes have the full right to choose and carry on any industry, profession, art, or craft.[91]

Given that these laws were passed by D'Annunzio himself in 1920 (when there was very little gender equality at all in European society), the accusations of misogyny directed at him are truly perplexing.

The rights Fiume conferred on its citizens extended even further than some contemporary democracies:

8. The Constitution guarantees to all citizens of both sexes: primary instruction in well-lighted and healthy schools; physical training in open-air gymnasiums, well-equipped; paid work with a fair minimum living wage; assistance in sickness, infirmity, and involuntary unemployment; old age pensions; the enjoyment of property legitimately obtained; inviolability of the home; 'habeas corpus'; compensation for injuries in case of judicial errors or abuse of power.[92]

Some of these declarations clearly arose from the influence of the socialists at Fiume. However, D'Annunzio nevertheless retained his nationalist beliefs as well and stated that "industries started or supported by foreign capital and all concessions to foreigners will be regulated by liberal legislation."[93] By combining his nationalist objectives with socialist principles, D'Annunzio once again sought to demonstrate that he was a leader for all of Fiume, and not just its Left or Right. The three articles of belief which took precedence over all others in Fiume stated that

> [l]ife is a good thing, it is fit and right that man, reborn to freedom, should lead a life that is noble and serious; a true man is he who, day by day, renews the dedication of his manhood to his fellowmen; labor, however, humble and obscure, if well done adds to the beauty of the world.[94]

Thus, even the lowest worker, if he leads a noble existence, adds to the beauty of D'Annunzio's civilization, because he assists in its creation. No citizen, no matter how minor, is denigrated in the Charter. Thus, the allegations that D'Annunzio regime was an oppressive one fall apart once his actual writings are studied.

Further into the Charter, those elements which were strictly 'D'Annunzian' in character begin to appear. On the surface, these appeal to the workers, but they also pave the way for an intellectual and artistic elite to emerge along the lines of a 'neo-Platonic' type of academy. Some of these ideas may drag the reader far out of his political comfort zone and into a world where arts and culture triumph over vulgar politics. It is via this line of thinking that D'Annunzio reverts to his influences from Nietzsche by emphasizing culture as the primary vessel of politics. This is an elaboration of Nietzsche's *Geisterkrieg*, which today is sometimes referred to as 'metapolitics.' Like Nietzsche, D'Annunzio believed that culture is the ultimate tool required to build a great nation and enact 'Grand Politics':

50. For any race of noble origin, culture is the best of all weapons.

For the Adriatic race, harassed for centuries by a ceaseless struggle with an unlettered usurper, culture is more than a weapon; like faith and justice, it is an unconquerable force.[95]

[…]

For the people of Fiume at the moment of her rebirth to liberty, it becomes the instrument more helpful than any other against the insidious plots that have encircled her for centuries.

Culture is the preservative against corruption; the buttress against ruin.

In Dante's Carnaro the culture of the language of Dante is the custodian of that which has ever been reckoned as the most precious treasure of the people, the highest testimony to the nobility of their origin, the chief sign of their moral right to rule.

That moral right is what the new State must fight for. On its will to victory is founded the exaltation of the human ideal.

The new State, with unity completed, liberty achieved, justice enthroned, must make it her first duty to defend, preserve, and fight for unity, liberty, justice in the spirit of man.

> The culture of Rome must be here in our midst and the culture of Italy.
>
> For this cause, the Italian province of Carnaro makes education – the culture of her people – the crown and summit of her Constitution, esteems the treasure of Latin culture as the foundation of her welfare.[96]

Fiume, then, if left to its own devices, would have brought the world a society based on culture and education. D'Annunzio intended to achieve this by providing free higher education. This, of course, is the opposite of most 'modern' societies, in which higher education comes with a lifetime of crippling levels of debt.

> 51. The city of Fiume will have a free University, housed in a spacious building, capable of accommodating a great number of students and ruled by its own special ordinances.

This isn't his only new educational policy, however, D'Annunzio also wanted all political and religious emblems removed from schools. Given D'Annunzio's views on politics, the banning of party propaganda wouldn't be surprising. However, banning religion seems contradictory, given the role that elements of religiosity played in his own style of governance:

> 54. Schools, well lighted and ventilated, must not have on their walls any emblems of religion or of political parties.

The public schools welcome the followers of every religious profession, the believers in every creed and those, too, who are able to live without an altar and without a God.[97]

There are three possible reasons for this proclamation. The first is that the citizens of Fiume had such a broad range of religions and political persuasions that D'Annunzio could not afford to risk promoting one group over another. The second is that he wished the students to be free from all kinds of persuasive dogma in order to develop their own 'inner Übermensch' and thus develop a culture of leaders instead of followers. The third possibility is that D'Annunzio himself did not adhere to any major religion and simply opted out of supporting any of them due to a personal interest in esotericism, as is hinted at below:

Others were enchanted with modern technology; D'Annunzio always wrote with a quill pen. Others were fascinated by the progress of science; D'Annunzio became a mystic, "reading" the cards in the evening, spending hours on end with witches and soothsayers, studying the secret meanings of numbers, learning the "wisdom of the Orient."[98]

Rumours of occult connections surrounded D'Annunzio, but even if true, they do not pertain to Nietzsche's influence. Though Nietzsche's views on Christianity are quite blatantly negative, Nietzsche had no interest in occult or esoteric practices, so this is a unique trait attributed to D'Annunzio. D'Annunzio also does not seem to have adopted Nietzsche's negative views on Christianity, and he often uses Christian symbolism in his work, such as the imagery of Saint Sebastian. Nevertheless, Don Celso Constantini, the apostolic administrator of Fiume, observed that "[t]he life of Fiume, agitated, tumultuous, torn by diverse political currents that were a mixture of idealism and materialism, was already sufficiently pagan without it being necessary to publicly proclaim a humanistic cult,"⁹⁹ and that D'Annunzio had contributed to a rebirth of a pagan cult in which hedonism and aesthetics took precedence over ethics "and Orpheus over Christ."¹⁰⁰

This interest in Dionysus again shows Nietzsche's influence. Apparently, Nietzsche was not the 'Last Priest of Dionysus,' as he once famously wrote; D'Annunzio seems to have accepted the challenge as a suitable replacement, for *Il fuoco* is full of glowing references to Dionysus:

> The Florid, the Fruit-bearer, the visible Remedy of mortals, the sacred Flower, the Friend of pleasure, Dionysus the liberator, suddenly reappeared before the face of man on the wings of song, crowning that nocturnal hour with bliss, incessantly holding out to the senses as in a full chalice all the good things of life.¹⁰¹

Stelio (who, as previously noted, represents D'Annunzio himself) refers to both the women in his life, Donatella and La Foscarina, as "Ariadne," and he writes that "Ariadne possesses a divine gift by which her power transcends all limits."[102] Nietzsche would also refer to his love interests as 'Ariadne', being the name of the fabled woman who helped Theseus against the Minotaur, only to be later abandoned by him and then marry the God Dionysus. Thus, both Nietzsche and D'Annunzio identified with the Hellenic Dionysus.

Whilst Constantini makes no reference to anti-Christian sentiments, he does describe a pro-pagan atmosphere in Fiume, although this could just be an innocent manifestation of D'Annunzio's interest in Hellenic history coupled with his theatrical style. The 'Dionysian atmosphere' may also refer to the 'festival' atmosphere D'Annunzio strove to evoke to keep the citizens entertained, which he also promulgated through musical performances.

The most famous feature of the Charter is its unique reference to music and the striking emphasis it places on it. Fiume, had it been allowed to develop, would have been a paradise for musicians. Music was considered to be on par with religious experience – which is perhaps another reason why Constantini was irate:

> 64. In the Italian province of Carnaro, music is a social and religious institution. Once in a thousand or two thousand years music springs from the soul of a people and flows on forever.

> A noble race is not one that creates a God in its own image but one that creates also the song wherewith to do Him homage.

Every rebirth of a noble race is a lyric force, every sentiment that is common to the whole race, a potential lyric; music, the language of ritual, has power, above all else, to exalt the achievement and the life of man.

Does it not seem that great music has the power to bring spiritual peace to the strained and anxious multitude?

The reign of the human spirit is not yet.

'When matter acting on matter shall be able to replace man's physical strength, then will the spirit of man begin to see the dawn of liberty': so said a man of Dalmatia of our own Adriatic, the blind seer of Sebenico.

As cock-crow heralds the dawn, so music is the herald of the soul's awakening.[103]

D'Annunzio saw music as a form of transcendence that could be used in the service of the state. Music was also of great importance to Nietzsche. As he once wrote, "by means of music the passions are expressed." Therefore, as with D'Annunzio, he believed music be the 'expression' or 'soul' of the nation. This renders music a potent weapon in culture's arsenal. By contrast, today's politicians have been slow to make use of musicians or artists, possibly because the current social emphasis is on capitalism, which by its very nature, erodes and stifles all artistic endeavors. Nietzsche understood its importance, however:

Nietzsche may well be the philosopher most often associated with music and, as Ernst Bertram has argued and Curt Paul Janz has demonstrated at length, Nietzsche's life was bound up with music. This is a literal claim in the case of Nietzsche, who played the piano with a passion and performative skill that captivated most of his contemporaries.[104]

Fiume's emphasis on music ties in with D'Annunzio's metaphysical view of the world, in which religious experiences were not restricted to church functions.[105] He believed art could evoke a mystical experience.

However, Gabrielle D'Annunzio's reign at Fiume was to be short-lived. Following the signing of the Treaty of Rapallo in December 1920, which sealed the city's fate, D'Annunzio was ousted by the Italian military, and by the end of the year, the equally short-lived Free State of Fiume was established in place of his government. Kochnitzky wrote in his memoirs that "the Socialist Party must bear a tremendous responsibility" for the failure of D'Annunzio's experiment."[106] This was an unfortunate consequence of their support for Fiume. According to Michael Leeden, while "men on the Right had urged caution and patience, those of the Left (in the form of the *Gente del mare*) had provided guns and a ship for Fiume, had undertaken a program of propaganda on Fiume's behalf within Italy, and were urging the *comandante* to ally with the revolutionary forces of the country."[107] In other words, the Italian government was under pressure to expel D'Annunzio from Fiume because the Socialists were providing him with arms, and there was a very real risk of D'Annunzio sparking a wide-scale political conflict within Italy itself. However, D'Annunzio did not blame the Socialists for his downfall at Fiume, but rather Mussolini, as he writes here in a rather terse fashion, insulting Mussolini for his lack of support:

> I am amazed at you...you tremble with fear! You stay there chattering, while we struggle... What about your promises? Can't you at least punch a hole in that belly that weighs you down, and deflate it?[108]

> Throughout his career, even before he became famous as a political activist and a soldier, D'Annunzio had divided the people of the world into two rough categories: those of the spiritual elite who were his friends and allies, and those reprobates who opposed his will.[109] Mussolini, despite his efforts to politically 'seduce' D'Annunzio, was never viewed by him as a friend or ally. D'Annunzio viewed Mussolini with skepticism and mistrust because Mussolini was brazenly stealing his ideas and then rebranding them as his own. D'Annunzio viewed this distasteful and found Mussolini's misappropriation of his aesthetics profoundly annoying. He now realized that Italian politics had taken a very sinister turn, and he wrote to de Ambris in February 1921 to lament that "[i]t is all corrupted. It is all gone astray."[110]

Later that year, in June, D'Annunzio sent a message to the Arditi reiterating his advice that they should hold themselves aloof from any existing political formation, by which he explicitly meant Fascism and Mussolini.[111] Eventually, after coming to power, Mussolini financed D'Annunzio's 'retirement' and kept him imprisoned at the Vittoriale. In a letter, D'Annunzio related that "I am a perpetual prisoner here."[112] And on March 1, 1938, D'Annunzio was found dead. Ernesto Cabruna, who was among his trusted lieutenants at Fiume, wrote of the events preceding D'Annunzio's death, predicting that

> [h]istory will reveal how Fascism diabolically kept D'Annunzio prisoner at the Vittoriale in the last years of his life […] D'Annunzio had twenty-one persons in his service, six of them were members of the Fascist police.[113]

Closure

It should be embarrassing that one of Italy's finest writers and national heroes has had to endure posthumous slander in the way that D'Annunzio has. Even more embarrassing is the shoddy scholarship which has led to this falsification of his history. D'Annunzio's writings have been nearly forgotten in the Anglophone world, his films buried, and his entire life ridiculed. Almost all contemporary articles about D'Annunzio are sensational and serve only to spread the slander about him to a new generation of readers whose knowledge of history is, at best, minimal. As Paolo Valesio says, "The literary injustice committed with regard to Gabriele D'Annunzio is the most flagrant of the twentieth century in Italy and perhaps in all of Europe."[114] Removing D'Annunzio from the literary canon is as pernicious as trying to erase Michelangelo from the history of art.

There is a substantial amount of common ground to be found between Nietzsche and D'Annunzio. The most prominent of these is D'Annunzio's interest in the Übermensch, which is a role he ascribes to many of his fictional characters, even though they sometimes struggle with mundane and earthly desires. D'Annunzio was also inclined towards aristocratic notions but lived in a time when the aristocracy was decadent, decaying, and reaching the end of its natural lifespan. However, he still saw its potential *if* it could be recreated as a system that wasn't merely based on birthright privilege. For D'Annunzio, aristocracy was – at least ideally – a way of living a vital Nietzschean life as a creator, an artist who uses civilization as a canvas to produce a great work of beauty. This emphasis on the arts and beauty is of crucial importance to understanding both Nietzsche and D'Annunzio, who both see art and culture as a means of transcending the world of the mundane and reaching a higher form of life.

D'Annunzio takes Nietzsche's conception of the artist-philosopher even further because he believes that the true Ideal (in the Platonic sense) for Italian civilization is Beauty – when D'Annunzio refers to himself as the 'Candidate for Beauty' he is, therefore, saying that he is the political candidate of Italy's *Zeitgeist*, a nation whose true soul is art, beauty, and refined culture. This is an interesting concept given the long and illustrious history of Italian art, especially when one recalls Julius Caesar's claim that he was a direct descendant of Aeneas, the son of Venus.

If Nietzsche was 'dynamite,' D'Annunzio was an atomic bomb. In Nietzsche's writings, it is quite clear that he hopes that others will come after him to follow the course he has charted and anticipates that his best readers will be in the future. D'Annunzio tried to do exactly this.

> The ideal and best readers are always (permanently) in the future, he claims that the presuppositions of the discipline require this conviction despite the recalcitrant fact that there are no (and that there have never been) instances of such readers apart from authors themselves, that is, "those who write, or could write, books of the same type."[115]

In this passage, we see a direct reference not only to readers but to *writers*: authors with ideas similar to Nietzsche's own. Nietzsche makes the purpose of these future authors clear when he writes:

> But one thing will live, the monogram of their very own essence, a work, a deed, an uncommon inspiration, a creation. That will live because no later world can do without it.[116]

Nietzsche expects that such authors would continue his work and leave their own mark on history. As an author, and as a man, D'Annunzio certainly fulfilled this hope by making a lasting imprint on history: he provided Italy with great literature as well as a great resurgence in national pride. If it were not for factors beyond his control, D'Annunzio would be more widely remembered as a great man today.

ENDNOTES

[1] D'Annunzio, G., *The Child of Pleasure* (New York: The Modern Library, 1925), Harding, G., & Symons, A., trans.

[2] Huges-Hallett, L., *Gabriele D'Annunzio: Poet, Seducer, and Preacher of War* (New York: Anchor Books, 2014), 7.

[3] Ibid., 3.

[4] Ibid., 6.

[5] Woodhouse, J., *Gabriele D'Annunzio: Defiant Archangel* (Oxford: Oxford University Press), 90.

[6] Hutter, H., *Shaping the Future: Nietzsche's New Regime of the Soul and Its Ascetic Practices* (Lanham, MD: Lexington Books, 2005), 96.

[7] Ibid., 100.

[8] Woodhouse, *Gabriele D'Annunzio*, 160.

[9] Huges-Hallett, *Gabriele D'Annunzio*, 10.

[10] Ledeen, M. A., *The First Duce: D'Annunzio at Fiume* (Baltimore, MD: The John Hopkins University Press, 1977), 5.

[11] Griffin, G., *Gabriele D'Annunzio: The Warrior Bard* (London: John Long Limited, 1935), 37.

[12] Babich, B. E., *Words in Blood, Like Flowers: Philosophy and Poetry, Music and Eros in Hölderlin, Nietzsche, and Heidegger* (Albany, NY: State University of New York Press, 2006), 39.

[13] Ibid., 39.

[14] Di Mauro-Jackson, M. M., *Decadence as a Social Critique in Huysmans, D'Annunzio, and Wilde* (Austin, TX: The University of Texas, 2008), 126.

15 Ibid., 141.

16 Ibid., 161-162.

17 Ibid., 131.

18 Ibid., 128.

19 D'Annunzio, *The Child of Pleasure*.

20 Ibid.

21 D'Annunzio, G., *Nocturne and Five Tales of Love and Death* (Marlboro, VT: The Malboro Press, 1988), trans. Rosenthal, R., 123.

22 Di Mauro-Jackson, *Decadence as a Social Critique in Huysmans, D'Annunzio, and Wilde*, 143.

23 Ibid., 164.

24 Huges-Hallett, *Gabriele D'Annunzio*, 174.

25 Di Mauro-Jackson, *Decadence as a Social Critique in Huysmans, D'Annunzio, and Wilde*, 161-162.

26 Huges-Hallett, L., *Gabriele D'Annunzio*, 176.

27 Woodhouse, J., *Gabriele D'Annunzi*, 29.

28 Ibid., 96.

29 Ibid., 247.

30 Woodhouse, *Gabriele D'Annunzio*, 188.

31 D'Annunzio, G., *The Flame of Life* (London: Forgotten Books, 2015), 18.

32 Ibid., 31.

33 D'Annunzio, *The Child of Pleasure*.

34 Woodhouse, *Gabriele D'Annunzio*, 118.

35 Ibid., 120.

36 Griffin, *Gabriele D'Annunzio*, 93.

37 Woodhouse, J., *Gabriele D'Annunzio: Defiant Archangel*, 128.

38 Hutter, *Shaping the Future*, 30.

39 Griffin, *Gabriele D'Annunzio*, 105.

40 Woodhouse, *Gabriele D'Annunzio*, 110.

41 Ibid., 111.

42 Nietzsche, *On the Use and Abuse of History for Life*.

43 Woodhouse, *Gabriele D'Annunzio*, 165

[44] Ibid., 163.

[45] Ibid., 10.

[46] Ledeen, *The First Duce*, 6.

[47] Huges-Hallett, *Gabriele D'Annunzio*, 204-205.

[48] Ibid., 205.

[49] Nietzsche, F., *The Will to Power* (New York: Random House, 1968), Kaufmann, W. & Hollingdale, R. J., trans, Kaufmann, W., ed., 71.

[50] Griffin, *Gabriele D'Annunzio,* 56.

[51] Ledeen, *The First Duce*, 6.

[52] Huges-Hallett, *Gabriele D'Annunzio*, 206.

[53] Ibid., 191.

[54] Woodhouse, *Gabriele D'Annunzio*, 207.

[55] Ibid., 111.

[56] Woodhouse, *Gabriele D'Annunzio*, 171.

[57] Huges-Hallett, *Gabriele D'Annunzio*, 54.

[58] Ibid., 201.

[59] Woodhouse, *Gabriele D'Annunzio*, 145.

[60] Griffin, *Gabriele D'Annunzio,* 11.

[61] D'Annunzio, *The Flame of Life,* 126.

[62] Valesio, P., *Gabriele D'Annunzio: The Dark Flame* (New Haven: Yale University Press, 1992), Migiel, M., trans., 24.

[63] Huges-Hallett, L., *Gabriele D'Annunzio: Poet, Seducer, and Preacher of War*, 393.

[64] Ledeen, *The First Duce*, 8.

[65] Huges-Hallett, *Gabriele D'Annunzio*, 53.

[66] Griffin, *Gabriele D'Annunzio,* 129.

[67] Ibid., 129.

[68] Ledeen, *The First Duce*, 17.

[69] Falasca-Zamponi, S., *Fascist Spectacle: The Aesthetics of Power in Mussolini's Italy* (USA: University of California Press, 2000), 6.

[70] Ledeen, *The First Duce*, 41.

[71] Huges-Hallett, *Gabriele D'Annunzio*, 440.

[72] Ibid., 395.

[73] Ibid., 378.

[74] Griffin, *Gabriele D'Annunzio*, 157.

[75] Huges-Hallett, *Gabriele D'Annunzio*, 415.

[76] Babich, *Words in Blood, Like Flowers*, 81.

[77] Ledeen, *The First Duce*, 150.

[78] Huges-Hallett, *Gabriele D'Annunzio*, 467.

[79] Ibid., 8.

[80] Ledeen, *The First Duce*, 71.

[81] D'Annunzio, *The Flame of Life*, 53.

[82] D'Annunzio, *Nocturne and Five Tales of Love and Death*, 229.

[83] Huges-Hallett, *Gabriele D'Annunzio*, 3.

[84] Ibid., 462.

[85] Ibid., 398.

[86] Bolton, K., *Artists of the Right: Resisting Decadence,* San Francisco: Counter-Currents Publishing Ltd., 2012), Johnson, G., ed., 27.

[87] Huges-Hallett, *Gabriele D'Annunzio*, 465.

[88] Ibid., 466.

[89] *Carta del Carnaro*, https://en.wikisource.org/wiki/Constitution_of_Fiume.

[90] Ibid.

[91] Ibid.

[92] Ibid.

[93] Ibid.

[94] Ibid.

[95] Ibid.

[96] Ibid.

[97] Ibid.

[98] Ledeen, *The First Duce*, 7.

[99] Ibid., 148.

[100] Ibid., 148.

[101] D'Annunzio, *The Flame of Life*, 80.

[102] Ibid., 283.

[103] *Carta del Carnaro*.

[104] Babich, *Words in Blood, Like Flowers*, 105.

[105] Ledeen, *The First Duce*, 150.

[106] Ledeen, *The First Duce*, 176.

[107] Ibid., 141.

[108] Huges-Hallett, *Gabriele D'Annunzio*, 422.

[109] Ledeen, *The First Duce*, 9.

[110] Huges-Hallett, *Gabriele D'Annunzio*,489.

[111] Huges-Hallett, *Gabriele D'Annunzio,* 491.

[112] Ibid., 510.

[113] Ibid.

[114] Valesio, *Gabriele D'Annunzio*, 1.

[115] Babich, *Words in Blood, Like Flowers,* 52.

[116] Nietzsche, *On the Use and Abuse of History for Life.*

www.ingramcontent.com/pod-product-compliance
Lightning Source LLC
Chambersburg PA
CBHW021918040426
42448CB00007B/810